CONTENTS

Unusual Animal Facts

1 The only bird that can fly backwards is the hummingbird.

2 The giant squid has the largest eyes in the world.

There's always one stray hummingbird in the flock who's got to show he can fly backwards

HHMMM HMMM HMMM HMMM

I'm sure I've never been down this end of the tank before!! Better go explore the new territory at the other end of the tank!

3 A goldfish has a memory span of three seconds.

4 A rat can survive longer without water than a camel.

1001 COOL FREAKY FACTS

with Glen Singleton

HB
HINKLER
BOOKS

1001 Cool Freaky Facts
Published in 2005 by Hinkler Books Pty Ltd
45-55 Fairchild Street
Heatherton VIC 3202 Australia
www.hinklerbooks.com

© Hinkler Books Pty Ltd 2005

Written by Nick Bryant
Illustrated by Glen Singleton
Edited by Julie Haydon
Cover design by Hinkler Books Design Studio

20 19 18 17 16 15
12 11 10

ISBN: 978 1 7412 1951 7

Typeset by Midland Typesetters, Maryborough, Victoria
Printed and bound in China

5 **T**oupees for dogs are sold in Tokyo.

6 **A** dolphin sleeps with one eye open.

7 **A** crocodile cannot stick its tongue out.

8 **A** mammal's blood is red, an insect's blood is yellow and a lobster's blood is blue.

9 **L**oud, fast music makes termites chew faster.

10 **A** blue whale's tongue weighs more than an elephant.

11 **A**n ostrich's eye is bigger than its brain.

12 **B**ats always exit a cave to the left.

13 **D**omestic cats kill an estimated one billion wild birds each year in the USA.

14 **T**igers have striped skin, not just striped fur.

The scene at the entrance to the batcave at rush hour.

Terry had to be careful in change rooms. For he had a secret. He was different from all the other tigers at school. Where they had stripes on their skin, ... Terry had spots!

15 **T**he blue whale's whistle is the loudest noise made by an animal.

16 **T**he heart of a giraffe weighs more than 11 kg (25 lb), is 60 cm (2 ft) wide and has walls 7.5 cm (3 in) thick.

17 **C**amels have three eyelids to protect their eyes from blown sand.

18 **A** mole can dig a tunnel over 90 m (300 ft) long in just one night.

Even though a blind mole can dig a tunnel up to 90 metres long ...that doesn't mean it knows where it's digging to!

19 **E**lephants are not afraid of mice.

Elephants are not afraid of mice, but are very afraid of the similar looking Rogue Rwandan Rockhopping Rodent.

Hi JUMBO!

20 **S**lugs have four noses.

21 **I**t is estimated that 25 per cent of cat owners blow-dry their pets.

22 **O**nly female mosquitoes bite.

23 **S**nakes are immune to their own venom.

24 **D**inosaurs probably lived to between 80 and 300 years of age. Scientists worked this out by looking at the structure of their bones.

25 **T**he fastest bird is the peregrine falcon. It can fly faster than 300 km (190 miles) per hour.

Excuse me Sir! Pull over and put the hand brake on. I clocked you travelling at over 300 kms per hour! Do you have a reason for that?

I'm a Peregrine Falcon Officer! That's what I do!

26 **I**n the Caribbean, there are oysters that can climb trees.

27 **M**osquitoes are attracted to the colour blue more than any other colour.

28 **C**ats cannot taste sweet things.

After 3 days of solid eating I haven't found one chocolate that tastes sweet yet...and I don't think I can stuff another one in!

29   **M**any species of reptiles have two penises.

30   **H**erons have been observed dropping insects on the water, then catching the fish that surface to eat the insects.

The not so smart Heron comes to the realisation that if dropping insects on the water attracts teensy weensy fish...it may also attract older hungrier not so friendly relatives as well.

31   **W**hen a mother cormorant feels her offspring are ready to leave the nest, she makes sure this happens by destroying the nest completely.

Oh brother! An ostrich egg! I can see why kids in Africa only ever ask for one boiled egg for breakfast!

32   **T**he largest egg is laid by the ostrich. An ostrich egg can be 20 cm (8 in) in length and 15 cm (6 in) in diameter.

33 The smallest egg is laid by the hummingbird. Its egg is less than 1 cm (0.39 in) in diameter.

34 A blind chameleon is still able to change the colour of its skin to match its environment.

35 Bald eagles can swim.

36 A zebra is white with black stripes, not black with white stripes.

37 The bird-eating spider from South America can have a legspan of 30 cm (1 ft).

38 Statistically you are more likely to be attacked by a cow than a shark.

39 An eagle can kill and carry an animal as large as a small deer.

40 At birth, a giant panda is smaller than a mouse.

41 A queen bee only uses her stinger to sting another queen bee.

42 An elephant's gestation period can be up to 22 months.

43 A chameleon's tongue is twice the length of its body.

44 To scare off enemies, the horned lizard squirts blood from its eyelids.

45 Spider silk, by weight, is stronger than steel.

46 A blue whale's heart only beats nine times per minute.

47 A hedgehog's heart beats 300 times per minute.

48 Horses can sleep standing up.

49 A cat needs four to five times more protein than a dog does.

50 When a baby kangaroo is born, it is about 2 cm (0.8 in) long.

51 An electric eel can produce a shock of 600 volts. That's enough to knock a horse off its feet.

52 Chimpanzees use tools more than any other animal, except humans.

The chimpanzees get some powertools for Christmas.

53 Lobsters can regenerate their legs, claws and antennae if these parts are pulled off by a predator.

54 **A** bald eagle's nest can be 3.65 m (12 ft) deep and 3 m (10 ft) wide.

55 **P**arrots live longer than any other type of bird. There are reliable reports of parrots living to 150 years of age.

56 **A**n African elephant has only four teeth.

57 **F**lying fish actually glide on wind currents. They can glide 6 m (20 ft) above the surface of the water.

58 **S**ea snakes are the most venomous snakes.

59 **A** scallop swims by quickly clapping its shell open and shut. This makes a water jet that pushes the scallop along.

60 Some captive octopuses have learned to open jars containing food. Many aquariums now give their octopuses puzzles and other games to keep them from getting bored.

Oscar, an octopus with plenty of time on his hands, contemplates an escape from the tank.

61 A fox will sometimes nip at the heels of cattle to make the cattle run. The cattle's stomping sends mice and other rodents out of the ground for the fox to eat.

62 The lungfish can live out of water for as long as four years.

63 Polar bears have been known to swim 100 km (62 miles) without stopping.

64 An ant can lift ten times its own weight.

65 The Egyptian vulture eats ostrich eggs. It uses stones to crack the eggshell.

66 Salamanders breathe through their skin.

67 Farmers in England are required by law to provide their pigs with toys.

68 A rhinoceros' horn is made of compacted hair.

69 A woodpecker can peck up to 20 times per second.

70 Kiwis mate for life. This can be up to 30 years.

71   Before seahorse eggs hatch, the male seahorse carries them in a pouch on his stomach.

72   A shark does not have bones. Its skeleton is made of cartilage.

73   Squirrels cannot remember where they have hidden half of their food.

74   The stegosaurus had a brain the size of a walnut.

It was always the Stegosauruses of the class that struggled in physics because of their walnut sized brain.

75   An octopus has three hearts.

76   The praying mantis is the only insect that can turn its head.

77 **A** penguin can drink salt water because it has a gland in its throat that removes the salt from the water.

78 **T**here are more plastic flamingos in the USA than real ones.

79 **A** giraffe has the same number of vertebrae in its neck as a mouse.

80 **T**urkeys often look up at the sky during a rainstorm. Unfortunately, some have drowned as a result.

81 **T**he Loch Ness monster is a protected animal under Scottish law.

82 **A** monkey was made a corporal in the South African army during World War II.

83 **A** snail can sleep for three years.

84 **A**n adult bear can run as fast as a horse.

85 **S**heep can recognise other sheep from photographs.

86 **A** locust can eat its own weight in food in one day. A typical person eats his weight in food in about six months.

87 **B**ees have five eyes.

88 Sharks kill about 40 people each year. This is a tiny number compared to the number of people that drown each year.

89 Honeybees kill more people than venomous snakes do.

90 Polar bears are left-handed.

91 Mosquito repellents do not repel. The repellent blocks a mosquito's sense of smell so it does not know a person is nearby.

92 A zebra foal can run with the herd an hour after its birth.

93 **A** marine catfish can taste with any part of its body.

94 **A** polar bear's fur is not white, but translucent.

95 **S**ome locusts have an adult lifespan of only a few weeks, after having lived in the ground as grubs for 15 years.

96 **B**utterflies taste with their feet.

97 **F**leas that live on rats have probably killed more people than anything else because they spread bubonic plague.

98   The polar bear is the only mammal with hair on the soles of its feet.

99   American President John Quincy Adams owned a pet alligator. He kept it in the East Room of the White House.

100   Female ants do all the work.

101   A cockroach can live up to two weeks with its head cut off before it starves to death.

102   Dogs can make about ten vocal sounds. Cats can make more than 100 vocal sounds.

103 **W**alruses turn pink if they stay out in the sun too long.

104 **M**ore animals are killed each year by cars than by hunters.

105 **A** beaver can hold its breath underwater for up to 45 minutes.

106 **T**here are 701 official breeds of dog.

107 **V**ultures have a unique defence mechanism; they throw up on their enemies.

108 **A** female pigeon cannot lay an egg unless she sees another pigeon. If another pigeon is not available, her own reflection in a mirror will do.

109 Female canaries cannot sing.

110 Cockroaches could survive a nuclear holocaust because radiation does not affect them as much as it affects other species.

111 The embryos of tiger sharks fight each other while in their mother's womb. Only the survivor is born.

112 Some lizards use their lungs to help them hear. Sound makes the lizard's chest vibrate. The vibrations are carried by air from the lungs to the lizard's head where they are heard.

113 Orang-utans protect their territory by burping loudly to warn off intruders.

114 Frogs can throw up. A frog throws up its stomach first, so that its stomach is dangling out of its mouth. Then the frog uses its forearms to dig out the stomach's contents. Then the frog swallows the stomach again.

115 Australian earthworms can grow up to 3 m (10 ft) in length.

116 Elephants and humans are the only animals that can stand on their heads.

No Eric! NOT THE CARTWHEEL!

Not to be content with being able to stand on his head... Eric the elephant attempted more difficult gymnastic exercises with disastrous consequences.

117 There is enough poison in a poison-arrow frog to kill 2200 people.

This isn't looking good... for me...or for whoever I'm being shot at.

118   **A** camel can drink up to 136 litres (30 gallons) of water at one time.

119   **R**ats and horses cannot vomit.

120   **R**acehorses can wear out new horseshoes in just one race.

121   **M**innows have teeth in their throat.

122   **I**f a starfish is cut into pieces, each piece will become another starfish.

123   **A** dolphin can hear sound underwater from 24 km (15 miles) away.

124 **A** scallop has 35 eyes.

125 **S**ome chimpanzees and orang-utans have been taught human sign language.

126 **M**ost insects are deaf.

127 **B**efore dolphins begin any group action, the pod holds a meeting. Each animal gets a chance to vocalise until a decision is made.

128 **S**nails produce a sticky discharge that forms a protective layer under them as they crawl. The discharge is so effective that a snail can crawl along the edge of a razor blade without cutting itself.

129 Earthworms have five hearts.

130 All pet hamsters are descended from one pregnant female found in the wild in 1930.

131 Some reptiles have eyes that operate independently of each other, so that the animal can see in two directions at once.

132 Groups of sea otters tie themselves together with kelp so they do not drift apart while they sleep.

133 A camel's hump stores fat, not water.

134 Neither emus nor kangaroos can walk backwards.

135 **C**ats hate lemons.

136 **T**he tusks of the woolly mammoth were 5 m (16 ft) long.

137 **A** daddy-long-legs spider is more venomous than a black widow spider but its fangs cannot penetrate human skin.

138 **C**amels will spit if annoyed.

139 **B**ees are born fully grown.

Ninety-one Funny Phobias

140 **A**blutophobia is the fear of bathing.

141 **A**carophobia is the fear of itching.

142 **A**gyrophobia is the fear of streets or crossing the street.

143 **A**lektorophobia is the fear of chickens.

Bob's irrational fear of chickens even went as far as the 5 PIECE CHICKEN MEAL DEAL (with a FREE DRINK)...at the local chicken takeaway.

144 **A**lliumphobia is the fear of garlic.

145 **A**mensiophobia is the fear of amnesia.

146 **A**nablepophobia is the fear of looking up.

147 **A**nemophobia is the fear of wind.

148 **A**peirophobia is the fear of infinity.

149 **A**rachibutyrophobia is the fear of peanut butter sticking to the roof of the mouth.

150 **A**utomysophobia is the fear of being dirty.

151 **B**arophobia is the fear of gravity.

152 **B**asiphobia is the fear of walking.

153 **B**ibliophobia is the fear of books.

154 **B**ogyphobia is the fear of bogeys or the bogeyman.

155 **B**romidrosi-phobia is the fear of body odour.

156 **C**haetophobia is the fear of hair.

157 **C**hrometophobia is the fear of money.

158 **C**hronophobia is the fear of time.

159 **C**linophobia is the fear of going to bed.

160 **C**oimetrophobia is the fear of cemeteries.

161 **C**oulrophobia is the fear of clowns.

162 **C**yberphobia is the fear of computers or working on computers.

163 **C**yclophobia is the fear of bicycles.

164 **D**ecidophobia is the fear of making decisions.

165 **D**oraphobia is the fear of fur.

166 **E**cophobia is the fear of home.

After being diagnosed with a fear of bicycles... twin brothers Eric and Edward... also known as 'The Bicycle Brothers'... resorted to other forms of wheeled transport... and felt much better for it.

167 **E**metophobia is the fear of vomiting.

No matter how hard they tried, Terry's friends could not make him vomit. For he had a fear of vomiting.

168 **G**eniophobia is the fear of chins.

169 **G**enuphobia is the fear of knees.

170 **G**eumaphobia is the fear of taste.

171 **G**nosiophobia is the fear of knowledge.

172 **G**ymnophobia is the fear of being naked.

173 **H**eliophobia is the fear of the sun.

174 **I**deophobia is the fear of ideas.

175 **K**leptophobia is the fear of stealing.

176 **K**oinoniphobia is the fear of rooms.

177 **K**oniophobia is the fear of dust.

178 **L**achanophobia is the fear of vegetables.

179 **L**eukophobia is the fear of the colour white.

180 **L**ogophobia is the fear of words.

181 **L**utraphobia is the fear of otters.

182 **M**acrophobia is the fear of long waits.

Mr Jones the friendly Station Master broke the bad news carefully to Edward (who had a fear of waiting) ...that his train service had been discontinued.

183 **M**eteorophobia is the fear of meteors.

184 **M**icrophobia is the fear of small things.

185 **M**nemophobia is the fear of memories.

186 **M**yrmecophobia is the fear of ants.

187 **M**yxophobia is the fear of slimy things.

188 **N**ebulaphobia is the fear of fog.

Fearing a thick fog entering his loungeroom and engulfing him while sleeping in front of the TV... ...Harold closed all doors and windows... but failed to close Harry the cat's cat flap in the back door.

189 **N**ephophobia is the fear of clouds.

190 **N**omatophobia is the fear of names.

191 **N**umerophobia is the fear of numbers.

192 **O**chophobia is the fear of vehicles.

A fear of vehicles drove Shirley to start a movement to bring back the HORSE for transport.

HORSE POWER is great! BRING BACK THE HORSE!

Give JOBS to out of work HORSES

I've been unemployed standing around eating grass in a paddock for five years!

193 **O**mbrophobia is the fear of rain.

Due to his irrational fear of rain, Alex spent two days pinned to a wall under an awning waiting for the low pressure storm cell to leave his country.

194 **O**mmetaphobia is the fear of eyes.

195 **O**rnithophobia is the fear of birds.

196 **P**agophobia is the fear of ice or frost.

197 **P**apyrophobia is the fear of paper.

198 **P**araskavedekatriaphobia is the fear of Friday the 13th.

199 **P**edophobia is the fear of children.

AHHRRR KIDS!

Driven by a fear of children...Mum climbed onto the chair. There was nowhere else to go... except up the wall from here!

ARRR AHHRR AAHHRR

200 **P**eladophobia is the fear of bald people.

201 **P**hagophobia is the fear of eating or swallowing.

202 **P**hilophobia is the fear of falling in love.

Esmerelda's fear of love was thinly disguised as a lack of interest.

203 **P**honophobia is the fear of noise.

204 **P**hotophobia is the fear of light.

205 **P**lutophobia is the fear of wealth.

206 **P**neumatophobia is the fear of air.

207 **P**ogonophobia is the fear of beards.

208 **P**teronophobia is the fear of being tickled with feathers.

209 **R**anidaphobia is the fear of frogs.

210 **R**ectophobia is the fear of rectums and rectal diseases.

211 **S**catophobia is the fear of fecal matter.

212 **S**elenophobia is the fear of the moon.

213 **S**omniphobia is the fear of sleep.

214 **S**ymmetrophobia is the fear of symmetry.

215 **S**yngenesophobia is the fear of relatives.

216 **T**aphephobia is the fear of being buried alive.

217 **T**eratophobia is the fear of monsters.

218 **T**onsurophobia is the fear of haircuts.

219 **T**remophobia is the fear of trembling.

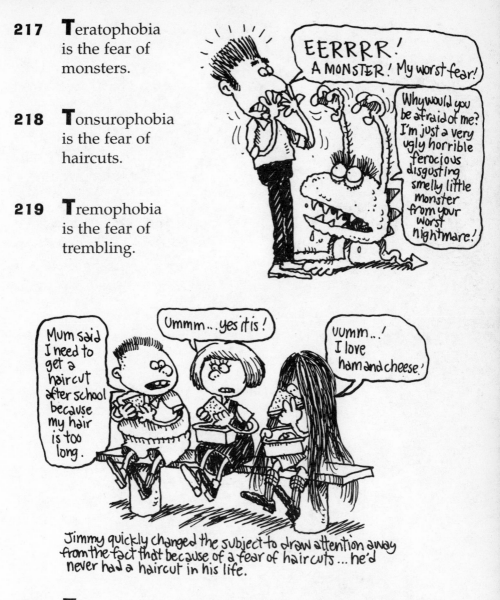

Jimmy quickly changed the subject to draw attention away from the fact that because of a fear of haircuts... he'd never had a haircut in his life.

220 **T**riskaidekaphobia is the fear of the number 13.

221 **U**ranophobia is the fear of urine or urinating.

222 **V**estiphobia is the fear of clothing.

223 **W**iccaphobia is the fear of witches and witchcraft.

224 **X**anthophobia is the fear of the colour yellow.

225 **X**enophobia is the fear of strangers or foreigners.

226 **Z**elophobia is the fear of jealousy.

227 **Z**emmiphobia is the fear of the great mole rat.

228 **Z**oophobia is the fear of animals.

And finally...

229 **P**hobophobia is the fear of fear.

230 **P**anophobia is the fear of everything.

George hid under his pillow when his fear of everything got to him...

Wacky World Records

If I could move my jaws to say it... I'd say... -89... Hey that's pretty cold!

VOSTOK...ANTARTICA 21st JULY 1983

231 The coldest temperature recorded on Earth was -89°C (-129°F) at Vostok, Antarctica, on 21 July 1983.

232 Charles Osborne had the hiccups for 69 years.

233 The world record for continuous pogo-stick jumping is 41 hours.

234 Bhutan was the last country to get the telephone. It did not have one until 1981.

235 The largest iceberg was sighted in the South Pacific Ocean in 1956. It was 332 km (208 miles) long and 96 km (60 miles) wide, or about the size of Belgium.

How much Ice did you need in your drink my dear?

I've brought back enough to cover Belgium.

236 The tallest tree in the world, a redwood, is 112 m (367 ft).

237 The longest kiss lasted 30 hours, 59 minutes.

238 The biggest palace in the world is the Imperial Palace in Beijing. It has so many rooms that you could sleep in a different room every night for 25 years.

Just imagine a treehouse up there!

239 The longest trip in a pedal boat was 7456 km (4660 miles).

240 Although covered with ice, Antarctica is the driest place on the planet with humidity lower than the Gobi Desert.

241 Every year 50 million cars are added to the world's roads. Car making is now the largest manufacturing industry in the world.

242 The longest time spent standing on one foot is 76 hours, 40 minutes.

243 In Great Britain, the most dangerous sport is gardening. Twenty per cent of all accidents there occur in the garden.

244 The biggest pumpkin weighed 449 kg (990 lb).

245 The warmest temperature recorded on Earth was 57.8°C (136°F) at El Azizia, Libya, on 13 September 1922. Bath water is considered scalding at 46°C (125°F).

246 The longest nose belonged to Thomas Wedders. It measured 19 cm (7.5 in). Thomas worked in a freak show in the 1770s.

247 The longest place name is 'Bangkok' in Thai. It is: Krungthep Mahanakhon Bovorn Ratanakosin Mahintharayutthaya Mahadilokpop Noparatratchathani Burirom Udomratchanivet Mahasathan Amornpiman Avatarnsathit Sakkathattiyavisnukarmprasit. It means 'City of Angels'. It is usually shortened to Krungthep Mahanakhon, for obvious reasons.

Mm! Mmmmm m m'mmm m mm OUCH! Mm mmm mm OUCH...mm mm mmmm (TRANSLATED)

Look! I'm going to have to call you back...OUCH! ...I'm in a competition trying to ...OUCH...stuff as many live scorpions into my mouth as I can.

248 The record for the most scorpions held in the mouth at one time is 20.

249 The first automobile race in the USA was held in Chicago in 1895. The track ran from Chicago to Evanston, Illinois. The winner was J. Frank Duryea, whose average speed was 12 km (7.5 miles) per hour.

250 The largest crater on the moon is also the largest impact crater in the solar system. It measures 2100 km (1300 miles) across.

251 Strongman John Evans holds the world record for the heaviest weight balanced only on his head. He balanced 101 bricks that weighed 188 kg (416 lb).

Ooh! Sorry! I figured it was only one more little brick!

Brian felt responsible for ruining John's world record attempt at balancing bricks on his head...by adding the 102nd brick.

252 The largest pearl ever found was the size of a tennis ball.

253 The fastest wind speed recorded was 508 km (318 miles) per hour in Oklahoma on 3 May 1999.

254 The largest known volcano is Olympus Mons on Mars. It is 590 km (370 miles) wide and 24 000 m (79 000 ft) high. It is almost three times higher than Mount Everest.

255 The Holy See (State of the Vatican City) in Rome, Italy, is the smallest sovereign state in the world. It has a population of less than 1000 people.

256 The youngest graduate got his bachelor's degree in 1994 at the age of ten years, five months.

257 Dorothy Straight's first book, *How The World Began*, was published in 1964 when she was six years old, making her the youngest ever published author.

258 The most powerful computer in the world is the ASCI White at the USA's Department of Energy. The computer incorporates 8192 x 375 Mhz processors, six terabytes of memory and 160 terabytes of disk storage. It is capable of processing 12.30 teraflops (trillions of operations per second).

259 The lightest person weighed 6 kg (13 lb) on her twentieth birthday.

260 Jon Brower Minnoch of Seattle weighed 634 kg (1400 lb) when he was admitted to hospital. After 16 months, Minnoch was discharged at 215 kg (476 lb).

261 The oldest cockroach fossil is about 280 million years old, which means the cockroach lived 80 million years before the first dinosaurs.

262 The loudest burp was 112 decibels (think jet aeroplane).

263 The record for holding one's breath underwater is 7.5 minutes.

264 The world record for pole sitting is 196 days on a 2.5 m (8 ft) pole.

265 The only time on record that snow has fallen in the Sahara Desert was on 18 February 1979. The storm lasted half an hour and the snow soon melted.

Abdul and his friend Ali didn't want to miss any of the brief half hour snow season over the Sahara Desert in 1979... so were ready to go.

266 Golf is the only sport that has been played on the moon.

267 The shortest war in history was fought between Zanzibar and England in 1896. The war had lasted for just 38 minutes when Zanzibar surrendered.

268 The longest recorded flight of a chicken is 13 seconds.

269 More baked beans are eaten in Great Britain than in any other country.

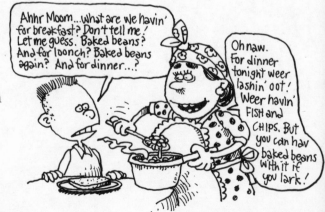

270 The world's smallest tree is the dwarf willow. It grows to 5 cm (2 in) on the tundra of Greenland.

A Greenlander about to flatten a whole forest of dwarf willows in one step!

271 The oldest known living thing is a bristlecone pine called Methuselah. It is located in the White Mountains on the California–Nevada border. The tree is estimated to be 4767 years old.

Hey Dad! Wait until you see what we've got! We've got us... A CHRISTMAS TREE!

Chucky brings home the 4767 year old Bristlecone pine after a hiking trip to the White Mountains of USA.

272 *The Guinness Book of Records* holds the record for being the book most often stolen from public libraries.

273 The world's youngest parents were eight and nine years old and lived in 1910.

274 **A**ir hostess Vesna Vulovic of Yugoslavia fell 10 160 m (33 330 ft) from an aeroplane into a snowbound forest in Serbska Kamenice, Czechoslovakia, on 26 January 1972. It was the longest fall a person has survived.

It's Only Natural

275 **W**atermelons are grown square in Japan so they take up less space and are easier to stack.

276 **A**n apple, potato and onion all taste sweet if you eat them with your nose plugged.

277 **J**upiter is bigger than all the other planets in our solar system combined.

278 Hot water is heavier than cold water.

279 Natural gas has no smell. The smell is added for safety reasons.

280 Research indicates that plants grow better when they are stroked.

I stroke my daisies every day and they're growing beautifully. But I don't know about you my prickly little friend.

While Olive stroked most of her plants to make them grow... Her very prickly cactii remained stunted in the corner of the greenhouse

281 Strawberries contain more vitamin C than oranges.

282 Forty-one per cent of the moon is not visible from Earth at any time.

No son. There's nobody on the moon. It's just a big hunk of dry rock revolving around the Earth that shines brightly at night.

Yes Captain Zardok ...we're ready to invade Earth on your command!

WHAT REALLY HAPPENS ON THE 41% OF THE MOON WE CAN'T SEE FROM EARTH.

283 Pollen never deteriorates. It is one of the few natural substances that lasts indefinitely.

284 A blue moon is the second full moon within a single calendar month.

285 The age of the universe is 13.7 billion years.

THE UNIVERSE TURNS 13·7 BILLION

286 Because of the rotation of the Earth, an object can be thrown farther if it is thrown west.

287 Ninety per cent of all extinct species are birds.

288 Sound travels through water three times faster than through air.

289 True berries include the grape, tomato and eggplant, but not the raspberry or blackberry.

290 **P**earls dissolve in vinegar.

291 **T**he largest flower in the world is the corpse flower or *Rafflesia*. It grows up to 1.2 m (4 ft) wide and it stinks.

292 **T**here are eight peas per pod on average.

293 **I**n Calama, a town in the Atacama Desert of Chile, it has never rained.

294 **R**aindrops are not really shaped like drops; they are perfectly round.

295 **L**emons contain more sugar than strawberries.

296 When scientists drilled through the ice of Antarctica's Lake Vanda, they discovered that the water at the bottom of the lake was an amazingly warm 24°C (77°F). Ice crystals heat the water by focusing light onto the bottom of the lake.

297 The Amazon rainforest makes one-fifth of the world's oxygen.

298 The Antarctic ice sheet contains 71 per cent of the world's fresh water.

Hmmm, Just smell that Amazon air!

sniff sniff

299 A tomato is a fruit, not a vegetable.

The Amazon rainforest makes ⅕ of the world's oxygen. What's not quite as well known is that it also makes a good percentage of the world's fish that can eat you... snakes that can crush you and natives that can kill you!

What fruit have you got in your lunchbox? I've got a banana!

Mum's given me an apple!

I've got a TOMATO! Did you know it was a fruit?

Freddy tried the... 'Did you know the TOMATO was a fruit trick' on his friends almost every week... and they were beginning to tire of it.

300 Lettuce is part of the sunflower family.

301 Water is the only substance on Earth that is lighter as a solid than as a liquid.

302 Coconuts kill more people than sharks do. Approximately 150 people are killed each year by coconuts.

303 Antarctica is the only place on Earth that is not owned by any country.

304 The liquid inside young coconuts can be used as a substitute for blood plasma.

305 The only food that does not spoil is honey.

306 Australia is the only continent on Earth without an active volcano.

307 **F**ingernails grow nearly four times faster than toenails.

308 **T**he apple, the almond and the peach are all members of the rose family.

309 **B**y raising your legs slowly and lying on your back, you cannot sink in quicksand.

310 **C**hina has a beverage called white tea. It is simply boiled water.

311 It is impossible to sneeze with your eyes open.

312 Venus is the only planet that rotates clockwise.

313 On 20 February 1943 in a cornfield near the village of Paricutin, Mexico, the ground cracked open and began to spew red-hot rocks. A volcano was born. It grew to 10.6 m (35 ft) the first day. By 1952, it had soared to 412 m (1352 ft) and had buried two towns.

314 The white oak does not produce acorns until it is about fifty years old.

Crunching Numbers

315 **B**uckingham Palace has more than 600 rooms.

316 **T**he opposite sides of a dice always add up to seven.

317 **W**oodpecker scalps, porpoise teeth and giraffe tails have all been used as money.

318 **A** bag of potato chips costs two hundred times more than the same weight in potatoes.

319 A jiffy is an actual unit of time. It is 1/100 of a second.

320 There are more than 600 million telephone lines in the world.

321 The average office worker uses about 10 000 sheets of paper each year.

322 Twenty per cent of all road accidents in Sweden involve a moose.

Twenty percent of all road accidents in Sweden involve a MOOSE.

323 There are more than 200 lashes on a human eyelid. Each lash is shed every three to five months.

324 More than 1000 languages are spoken in Africa.

325 **A**n ostrich egg takes four hours to hard-boil.

326 **A** porcupine has about 30 000 quills.

327 **M**ore than 50 billion aspirins are sold each year.

328 **H**umans have 639 muscles, but caterpillars have more than 4000.

329 **I**f you could drive to the sun at 90 km (55 miles) per hour, it would take about 193 years.

330 **E**very five seconds, a baby is born.

331 **Z**ippers are produced all over the world at a rate of 45 km (28 miles) per hour.

332 Just twenty seconds' worth of fuel remained when Apollo 11's lunar module landed on the moon.

All it took was a twenty second dispute over where to land to turn the first landing on the moon into the first crash on the moon!

333 Up to 25 cm (10 in) of rain can fall on a rainforest in a single day.

334 A solar day on Mercury, from sunrise to sunset, lasts about six Earth months.

335 The amniotic fluid that surrounds a baby in the womb is completely replaced every three hours.

336　There are more than 14 000 varieties of rice.

337　Cats can spend 16 hours a day sleeping.

338　A bee needs to flap its wings 250 times per second to remain in the air.

After what amounted to sleeping most of the day, Harry the Persian slept most of the night catching up on the sleep he missed during the day.

339　About 36 million phone calls are made each day in New York City.

340　It takes 72 muscles to speak one word.

341　In the first eight months of his presidency, George W. Bush was on vacation 42 per cent of the time.

342   An alligator has 80 teeth.

343   It takes approximately 850 peanuts to make a standard jar of peanut butter.

344   There are about five million grains in a packet of sugar.

345   The Great Wall Of China is 3460 km (2149 miles) long.

346   Summer and winter on Uranus each last 21 Earth years.

347   Forty-seven Bibles are sold every minute.

348 Each year about $200 million of American stamps go into the albums of 22 million stamp collectors.

349 McDonald's make 40 per cent of their profits from Happy Meals.

350 The weight of all the bacteria on Earth is estimated to be the weight of the United Kingdom.

351 There are 2.5 million rivets in the Eiffel Tower.

352 The Earth travels around the sun at about 107 000 km (67 000 miles) per hour.

Pierre the Rivet Counter at the Eiffel Tower loses count while counting rivets ...

353 The burrowing rate of the gopher is equivalent to a human digging a tunnel 45 cm (18 in) wide and 11 km (7 miles) long in ten hours.

354 Close to three billion movie tickets are sold in India every year.

355 One in five children in the world has never been inside a schoolroom.

356 One ragweed plant can release one billion grains of pollen per year.

357 On average, 18 acres of pizza are eaten every day in the USA.

358 A dragonfly lives for one day.

359 There are more insects in a 1.6 km (1 mile) square of rural land than there are people on the planet.

A dragonfly lives for one day...
...that's 24 hours...
WHOOPS! Time's up!

DON'T MOVE SHIRLEY OLD GIRL!
Do you realise that if you do....
you might squash more bugs than there are people in China!

360 The largest American bill is for $100 000.

361 The human heart creates enough pressure to squirt blood over 9 m (30 ft).

Oh...what did you do to yourself?
You've cut your finger!
Let's get a dressing on that little bleeder.

362 A dairy cow will give about 200 000 glasses of milk in its lifetime.

363 Chamoy Thipyaso was convicted of fraud and sentenced to 141 078 years in a Thai prison.

364 The main library at Indiana University sinks over 2.5 cm (1 in) every year. When it was built, engineers failed to take into account the weight of the books that would occupy the building.

The library at Indiana University finally sinks under the weight of the books after C.J. returns his three overdue library books.

INDIANA UNIVERSITY LIBRARY

It was only two pretty light paperbacks and a comic book!

Ahhr...I'm sorry Sir, but your pack of chewing gum is scanning up here as a $9 bag of potatoes. Is that OK with you? Does it look like a bag of potatoes to you?

POTATOES $9.00

BEEP

365 The first product to have its barcode scanned was a pack of Wrigley's gum.

366 There are 18 doctors in the USA called Dr Doctor, and one called Dr Surgeon.

367 One 75-watt bulb gives more light than three 25-watt bulbs.

368 Twenty thousand men took 22 years to build the Taj Mahal.

369 Bolivia has two capital cities.

370 The American government has nearly 7.5 billion grams of gold tucked away. Most of it is at Fort Knox.

371 A Weddell seal can hold its breath underwater for seven hours.

372 In America, every major league baseball team buys about 20 000 baseballs a year.

373 The height of the Eiffel Tower varies by as much as 15 cm (6 in), depending on the temperature.

374 Mickey Mouse received 800 000 pieces of fan mail in 1933.

MICKEY MOUSE READS HIS FAN MAIL

375 The blue whale, the largest animal ever, is 30 m (100 ft) long. It weighs as much as 4 large dinosaurs, 23 elephants, 230 cows or 1800 men.

376 The name Hitler was listed 22 times in the New York phone book before World War II. After the war, the name was not listed once.

377 Almost one-quarter of all mammal species on Earth are bats.

Bats make up one quarter of all mammals on Earth...
And Juan finds the cave in Bolivia where they all live.

378 Lightning is five times hotter than the surface of the sun.

379 The average American over fifty will have spent five years waiting in lines.

380 The Earth is 4.5 billion years old.

381 The search engine Google got its name from the word 'googol', which is the number one with a hundred zeros after it.

382 The largest hotel in the world in 2002 was the MGM Grand in Las Vegas, Nevada, with 5034 rooms.

383 Wearing headphones can increase the bacteria in your ears by up to 700 times.

384 The leaves of some water lilies can be 2.4 m (8 ft) wide.

385 It takes about 63 000 trees to make the Sunday edition of the *New York Times*.

386 It takes nearly 2500 cows to supply the USA's National Football League with enough leather to make a year's supply of footballs.

387 In Haiti, only one out of every 200 people owns a car.

388 Pain travels through the human body at a speed of over 106 m (350 ft) per second.

389 The sun makes up 99 per cent of the matter in our solar system.

390 The weight of all the insects on Earth is twelve times greater than the weight of all the people on Earth.

391 The average person spends three years of their life on the toilet.

392 There are approximately 3500 astronomers in the USA, but more than 15 000 astrologers.

393 The average number of people in aircraft over the USA in any given hour is 61 000.

394 **A** person drinks about 75 000 litres (20 000 gallons) of water in his lifetime.

395 **T**he human head contains 22 bones.

After hearing that a person drinks 75,000 litres of water in a lifetime... Arnold decided to drink all of his share in one go and get it over and done with.

396 **L**ightning strikes the Earth 100 times every second or 6000 times every minute.

397 **Y**ou share your birthday with more than nine million people.

398 **O**ne bat can consume 1000 mosquitoes in a single hour.

399 **A**n office desk has 400 times more bacteria on it than a toilet does.

400 The average lead pencil can be used to draw a line 56 km (35 miles) long or to write approximately 50 000 English words.

50 kms. into his 56 km line Al's pencil began to run low... But fortunately for Al he had a spare pencil to finish the last 6 kms of his line. And why was he drawing a 56 km line? Well...it was easier than writing 50,000 words the the average pencil is good for....

401 The wingspan of a Boeing 747 is longer than the Wright brothers' first flight.

402 By weight, a hamburger costs more than a new car.

403 No piece of dry, square paper can be folded in half more than seven times.

404 More than two billion pencils are manufactured each year in the USA. If these were placed end to end they would circle the world nine times.

405 Recycling one glass jar saves enough energy to power a television for three hours.

After learning on TV that recycling one glass jar could power a television for one hour... Debbie figured that gobbling down a jar of pickled onions.. a jar of anchovies and a half jar of pickled gherkins would give her at least a full day of TV.

406 If all the blood vessels in your body were placed end to end, they would make a line about 96 000 km (60 000 miles) long.

407 In one day your heart beats 100 000 times.

408 At a steady jogger's pace of 10 km (6 miles) per hour, it would take 173 days to go around the equatorial circumference of Earth, and more than five years to go around Jupiter, the largest planet.

OUCH! It's my sore toe. I can't go on!

Herb was forced to abandon his 173 day training run around the world after only 10 minutes blaming an ingrown toenail as the reason. His coach and manager feared his problem toe may act up on his 5 year run around the planet Jupiter.

409 The Empire State Building consists of more than ten million bricks.

410 The longest conga had 119 986 people in it.

411 There are more than 3500 living species of cockroaches.

After the dust had settled... King Kong counted some of the 10 million bricks that once made up the Empire State Building.

412 The average bank teller loses about $250 every year.

413 A human's small intestine is 6 m (20 ft) long.

414 Scientists estimate that there are at least 15 million stars for every person on Earth.

415 **A** car travelling at 160 km (100 miles) per hour would take more than 29 million years to reach the nearest star beyond the sun.

416 **T**here are ten towns named Hollywood in the USA.

417 **S**ome kinds of bamboo grow 89 cm (35 in) in one day.

418 **I**t is estimated that 6800 languages are spoken in the world today.

419 **I**n the average lifetime a person will breathe in nearly 20 kg (44 lb) of dust.

420 **Y**ou blink over ten million times in a year.

421 The most drought-resistant tree is the boab tree. It can store 163 000 litres (35 800 gallons) of water in its trunk for later use.

CHOP
CHOP
GUSH

It was while chopping firewood in the Outback that Jack discovered the difference between a gumtree and a Boabtree is about 163,000 litres of water.

422 Three hundred and fifteen entries in Webster's 1996 dictionary were misspelled.

423 Rats multiply so quickly that in 18 months, two rats could have more than one million descendants.

I'm sorry to say dear...
And I don't know how to tell you this...
But I think we've got a
RAT PROBLEM!
Our family has..... well...
bred like rats!

I know!
There must be a
million of them!
I lost track of their
names after the
first couple of
hundred thousand!

424 A butterfly has more than 12 000 lenses in each eye.

425 There are more telephones than people in Washington, DC.

426 The combined wealth of the world's 250 richest people is greater than the combined wealth of the poorest 1.5 billion people.

427 The first number plates were introduced in 1893.

428 Outer space begins 80 km (50 miles) above the Earth.

Oh I say! That chap's speeding! Did you get his number plate?

ONE

Reginald Smith pays big money for the first number plate in 1893 and receives the first speeding ticket soon after.

429 When awake, cats spend up to 30 per cent of their time grooming.

Rex...always an excessive cat as a kitten, was not content with the average 30% of his time spent grooming... He went for the full 100%

430 A woodchuck breathes only ten times per hour while hibernating. An active woodchuck breathes 2100 times per hour.

431 An elephant
can smell
water nearly
5 km
(3 miles)
away.

432 Linen can
absorb up to
20 times its
weight in
moisture
before it
feels damp.

DRINKIES! YIPPEE!

It's hard to believe anyone can get so excited over dirty muddy river water.

WATERHOLE 5 km

It must be the African heat!

433 During a typical human life, a heart will beat
approximately 2.5 billion times.

434 In 1956, 80 per cent of American households had a
refrigerator compared to only eight per cent of
British households.

435 A hippo-
potamus
can open
its mouth
1.2 m (4 ft)
wide.

I was reading a magazine in a doctor's waiting room that a hippopotamus can open its mouth 1.2 metres wide... That's 4 feet! Wide enough to fit in an explorer or two... a canoe... two native porters and a cheeseburger.

436 The sperm
whale's
intestines
are over
137 m (450 ft) long.

437 Nicaragua had 396 different rulers between 1839 and 1855; their average reign lasted less than 15 days.

438 Each year lightning starts about 10 000 fires in the USA.

439 Each year chickens lay 400 billion eggs.

440 A human sneeze exits the mouth at almost 480 km (300 miles) per hour. This is the speed of the wind in a class five tornado.

441 There is the same amount of water in 25 cm (10 in) of snow as in 2.5 cm (1 in) of rain.

442 The fastest moon in our solar system circles Jupiter once every seven hours. It travels faster than 112 000 km (70 000 miles) per hour.

443 The largest jellyfish ever found was 2.3 m (7.5 ft) long.

444 A Boeing 747 aeroplane holds 260 000 litres (57 285 gallons) of fuel.

445 Besides inventing the telephone, Alexander Graham Bell set a world water speed record of 113 km (70 miles) per hour in a hydrofoil boat.

446 The estimated number of M&Ms sold each day in the USA is 200 million.

447 There are approximately 31.5 million seconds in a year.

448 It takes six months to build a Rolls Royce and 13 hours to build a Toyota.

449 The moon has no atmosphere, so footprints left there by astronauts should remain for at least ten million years.

450 The oldest fish in captivity lived to 88 years of age.

451 If you stretch out a standard slinky, it measures 26.5 m (87 ft).

452 Around ten per cent of all the people who ever lived are alive today.

453 On average, 100 people choke to death on ballpoint pens every year.

454 There are 2 598 960 five-card hands possible in a 52-card deck of cards.

455 The cruise liner, the QE2, moves only 15 cm (6 in) for each 4.5 litres (1 gallon) of diesel that it burns.

Entertain- ment and the Arts

456 When an orange is shown in any of *The Godfather* movies, it means a character is about to die or have a close call.

457 'Twinkle Twinkle Little Star' was written by Mozart.

458 When young and poor, Pablo Picasso kept warm by burning his own paintings.

It's my greatest work yet.'
It's about lots of little stars twinkling brightly in the sky at night over Austria. Something kids can sing along to. I'll call my masterpiece... TWINKLE TWINKLE LITTLE STAR.

After gazing at the night sky for ten minutes Mozart comes up with a great idea.

459 The first time a toilet was shown on television was in the show 'Leave It to Beaver'.

460 Charlie Chaplin once received 73 000 pieces of fan mail in three days.

461 Director George Lucas had trouble getting funding for the movie *Star Wars* because most film studios thought people would not go and see it.

462 No one knows where Mozart is buried.

463 Mel Blanc, who was the voice of Bugs Bunny, was allergic to carrots. He had to chew a carrot for a take, then spit it into a bucket.

464 Leonardo da Vinci spent 12 years painting *Mona Lisa*'s lips.

465 **W**alt Disney was afraid of mice.

466 **B**arbie's full name is Barbara Millicent Roberts.

467 **T**he first toy advertised on television was Mr Potato Head.

468 **B**ecause metal was scarce, the Oscars given out during World War II were made of wood.

469 **S**herlock Holmes never said 'Elementary, my dear Watson'.

470 **T**he most popular movie star in 1925 was the dog Rin Tin Tin.

471 **M**arcel the monkey was fired from the television show 'Friends' because of his nasty habit of vomiting live worms.

472 **S**occer is the most popular sport in the world.

473 **P**inocchio is Italian for 'pine eyes'.

474 **T**he shortest television commercial was one-quarter of a second long.

475 **'W**hite Christmas' sung by Bing Crosby has sold over 100 million records, making it the most popular recording of all time.

476 In 1935, a writer named Dudley Nichols refused to accept the Oscar for his screenplay *The Informer* because the Writers' Guild was on strike.

477 In 1970, George C. Scott refused the Best Actor Oscar for *Patton*.

478 In 1972, Marlon Brando refused the Oscar for his role in *The Godfather*.

479 In *Casablanca*, Humphrey Bogart never said 'Play it again, Sam'.

480 Donald Duck comics were once banned in Finland because Donald does not wear pants.

Donald Duck receives pants from fans in Finland to stop bans on his comics....

481 *Tom Sawyer* was the first novel written on a typewriter.

Author Mark Twain gives up the fountain pen and wrestles with new technology.

482 The largest book ever published is *Bhutan: A Visual Odyssey Across the Kingdom*. The book is 1.5 x 2.1 m (5 x 7 ft). It has 112 pages and weighs 60 kg (133 lb).

483 In Mel Brooks' *Silent Movie*, mime Marcel Marceau is the only person who has a speaking role.

484 The Bible has been translated into Klingon.

485 Boxing is the most popular theme in movies about sport.

Max makes a big mistake in believing the movie 'The Ring' was going to be a fantasy.

486 The world's longest-running play is *The Mousetrap*. It is a murder mystery that was written by Agatha Christie in 1947. It has been performed over 20 000 times.

487 In the 1991 Disney film *Beauty and the Beast*, one sign in the forest points to a place called Anaheim. Another sign points down a dark, sinister-looking path to Valencia. Anaheim is actually the site of Disneyland, while the rival Six Flags Magic Mountain amusement theme park is in the city of Valencia.

488 The first four countries to have television were England, the USA, the USSR and Brazil.

THE DAY **BEFORE** TELEVISION STARTED IN BRITAIN.

489 Donald Duck's middle name is Fauntleroy.

490 The song 'Rudolph the Red-Nosed Reindeer' was invented in 1939 for a department store promotion.

491 'The Muppet Show' was banned in Saudi Arabia because one if its stars was a pig.

492 Alfred Hitchcock did not have a belly button. It was eliminated when he was sewn up after surgery.

493 Virginia Woolf wrote all her books standing up.

494 The characters Bert and Ernie on 'Sesame Street' were named after Bert the cop and Ernie the taxi driver in Frank Capra's *It's a Wonderful Life*.

495 Before the 1960s, men with long hair were not allowed to enter Disneyland.

496 One of the biggest box-office flops was Kevin Costner's *Waterworld*, which cost more than $200 million.

497 Whoopi Goldberg's real name is Caryn Elaine Johnson.

498 Drew Carey once worked at Denny's.

499 The King of Hearts is the only king in a deck of cards with a moustache.

Nigel found to his surprise that in the deck of cards only the King of Hearts had a moustache. So with a quick flick of the felt pen ...everyone had a moustache ...and eyes...and hair...lots of hair...all of it black.

500 Mark Twain, one of America's best-loved authors, dropped out of school when he was 12 years old, after his father died.

501 Dolly Parton once lost a Dolly Parton lookalike contest.

502 In 1938, the creators of Superman sold the rights to the character for $65 each.

503 During the chariot scene in *Ben Hur* a small red car can be seen in the background.

Mario takes a wrong turn into the supermarket carpark and parks his little red car on the set of Ben Hur instead.

504 There were 47 Charlie Chan movies. Six different actors played the role but none of them were Chinese.

505 Vincent Van Gogh only sold one painting in his life and that was to his brother.

506 Debra Winger was the voice of ET.

507 More Monopoly money than real money is printed in a year.

508 The first time a toilet was flushed in a movie was in *Psycho*.

509 **S**onny and Cher originally called themselves Caesar and Cleo.

510 **I**n Finland, Cinderella is known as Tuna.

511 **X**-rays of the *Mona Lisa* show that there are three completely different versions, all painted by Leonardo da Vinci, under the final portrait.

X-Rays of the Mona Lisa reveal previous versions underneath!

512 **W**arren Beatty and Shirley Maclaine are brother and sister.

513 **T**he sound effect of ET walking was made by someone squishing jelly in her hands.

514   Every time Beethoven sat down to write music, he poured cold water over his head.

515   The longest non-talking film ever made was Andy Warhol's *Sleep*. It consists solely of a man sleeping for eight hours.

516   The quietest piece of music in the world is John Cage's '3 minutes and 27 seconds', which consists of a person sitting in front of a piano for that length of time, then leaving.

517   Leonardo da Vinci could write with one hand and draw with the other at the same time.

It's well known that Leonardo Da Vinci could use both hands at the same time to write and draw... but he may have also been able to balance a small leather ball on his nose while tapping his foot to Italian folk tunes as well.'

518 The first CD pressed in the USA was Bruce Springsteen's 'Born in the USA'.

519 During the eighteenth century, books that were considered offensive were sometimes whipped.

520 The idea of a countdown before a rocket launch originated as a tension-building device in the 1929 movie *The Woman on the Moon*.

521 The people of Iceland read more books per capita than any other people in the world.

522 In every episode of 'Seinfeld', there is a Superman.

523 The name of Oz in the *Wizard of Oz* was thought up by the creator, Frank Baum, when he looked at his filing and saw O-Z.

What the WIZARD OF OZ might have been called if Frank hadn't taken a few minutes more to think about the title and not glanced upon the O-Z file of his filing cabinet.

524 The first film with spoken dialogue premiered on 6 October 1927 in New York. It was *The Jazz Singer* starring Al Jolson.

525 John Travolta turned down the starring roles in *An Officer and a Gentleman* and *Tootsie*.

526 Whoopi Goldberg was a mortuary cosmetologist and a bricklayer before becoming an actress.

527 **M**any of the details we associate with Santa Claus were invented for a Coca Cola advertising campaign around 1890.

528 **I**n most television commercials that show milk, advertising milk (a mixture of white paint and a little thinner) is used in place of real milk.

529 **H**umphrey Bogart was related to Princess Diana. They were seventh cousins.

530 **T**he longest movie runs for 85 hours and is fittingly titled *The Cure for Insomnia*.

Sixty-nine Ludicrous Laws

Many of these laws date back to a time when the ideals they represented were commonly accepted. Some are still in place today because the local authorities have not bothered to remove them yet.

531 **P**acific Grove, California: It is a misdemeanour to kill or threaten a butterfly.

532 **V**entura County, California: Cats or dogs cannot mate without a permit.

Don't touch the butterfly dear! We don't want you doing time in a state run penitentiary with hardened criminals! Remember we have tough butterfly laws in th state.

533 **S**arasota, Florida: It is illegal to wear swimwear while singing in a public place.

534 **I**llinois: It is illegal to give lighted cigars to dogs, cats or other pets.

535 **C**hicago, Illinois: A hatpin is considered a concealed weapon.

536 **F**lorida: Men may not be seen publicly in any kind of strapless gown.

537 **B**elgium: Every child must learn the harmonica at primary school.

538 **F**lorida: If an elephant is left tied to a parking meter, the parking fee has to be paid.

539 **M**innesota: It is illegal to mock skunks.

540 **M**ichigan: It is illegal for a woman to cut her hair without her husband's consent.

541 **F**lorida: Unmarried women are prohibited from parachuting on Sundays.

542 **A**labama: It is illegal to wear a fake moustache that causes laughter in church.

Despite sitting in the very back row of the church... Charlie realised he'd been sprung wearing a fake moustache.

543 **B**ellingham, Washington: It was once illegal for a woman to take more than three steps backwards while dancing.

544 **B**rainerd, Minnesota: Every man must grow a beard.

545 **O**hio: It is illegal to sell beer while wearing a Santa Claus suit, even if you are a dog.

546 **S**eattle, Washington: It is illegal to sell lollipops, but suckers are fine.

547 **V**irginia: All bathtubs must be outside, not in the house.

548 **T**oronto, Canada: It is illegal to ride streetcars on Sundays after eating garlic.

549 **I**ndiana: People are not allowed to attend a movie house or theatre, nor ride in a public streetcar less than four hours after eating garlic.

550 Los Angeles: In 1838, a man had to obtain a licence before serenading a woman.

551 Cleveland, Ohio: It is illegal to capture mice without a hunting licence.

552 Arizona: It is illegal to hunt camels.

553 Kentucky: It is illegal to carry an ice-cream cone in your pocket.

554 Louisiana: It is illegal to rob a bank, then shoot the teller with a water pistol.

555 Indiana: It is prohibited to take a bath in the winter.

556 **K**entucky: You must take a bath at least once a year.

557 **A**laska: It is illegal to look at or pursue a moose from a flying vehicle.

558 **A**tlanta, Georgia: It is illegal to tie a giraffe to a telephone pole or street lamp.

559 **I**daho: It is forbidden to give a person a box of candy that weighs more than 23 kg (50 lb).

560 **N**ew York State: It is illegal to shoot a rabbit from a trolley car.

561 **S**omalia, Africa: It is illegal to carry old gum on the tip of your nose.

562 New Jersey: It is illegal to slurp soup.

563 Milan, Italy: Citizens can be fined $100 if seen in public without a smile on their face. Exemptions include time spent visiting patients in hospitals or attending funerals.

564 Vermont: Women must obtain written permission from their husbands to wear false teeth.

565 Asheville, North Carolina: It is illegal to sneeze on city streets.

566 Oklahoma: People who make ugly faces at dogs may be fined and jailed.

567 Arkansas: A man is allowed to beat his wife, but no more than once a month.

568 Chicago, Illinois: It is illegal for a woman who weighs more than 91 kg (200 lb) to ride a horse while wearing shorts.

569 San Francisco: It is illegal to use old underwear to clean cars in a car wash.

570 A few years ago, a city council member in Albuquerque tried to have Santa Claus banned from the city. He failed.

571 San Francisco: There is a ban on any mechanical device that reproduces obscene language.

572 **A**ncient Egypt: The penalty for killing a cat, even by accident, was death.

573 **N**ew York: It is illegal to have a puppet show in your window.

574 **S**an Francisco: Sneezing powders and stink balls are prohibited.

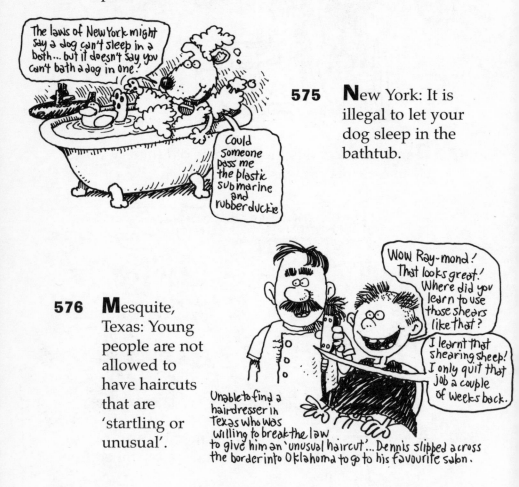

The laws of New York might say a dog can't sleep in a bath... but it doesn't say you can't bath a dog in one!

Could someone pass me the plastic submarine and rubber duckie

575 **N**ew York: It is illegal to let your dog sleep in the bathtub.

576 **M**esquite, Texas: Young people are not allowed to have haircuts that are 'startling or unusual'.

Wow Ray-mond! That looks great! Where did you learn to use those shears like that?

I learnt that shearing sheep! I only quit that job a couple of weeks back.

Unable to find a hairdresser in Texas who was willing to break the law to give him an 'unusual haircut'... Dennis slipped across the border into Oklahoma to go to his favourite salon.

577 **F**airbanks, Alaska: It is illegal to give a moose a beer.

578 **W**ashington State: Fake wrestling is not permitted.

KILLER and KARLA KOX the family wrestling team leave the casualty ward after a wrestling match in Seattle.

579 **T**urkey: In the sixteenth and seventeenth centuries, anyone caught drinking coffee was put to death.

580 **R**ussia: During the time of Peter the Great, any man who wore a beard had to pay a special tax.

581 **F**lorida: It is illegal to doze off under a hairdryer.

582 **G**eorgia: It is illegal to slap an old friend on the back.

Sgt. Smith kept mentioning it being illegal to nod off under a drier as Delores fought back sleep at the hairdressers.

583 Missouri: It is illegal to play hopscotch on a Sunday.

584 Boston: In the nineteenth century, it was illegal to bathe without a doctor's prescription.

585 Connecticut: It is illegal to walk across the street on your hands.

586 Avignon, France: It is illegal for a flying saucer to land in the city.

A scene in the night sky over Avignon, France where it's illegal for flying saucers to land....

You must understand. You cannot land here in our city of Avignon you dirty space dogs!

Go land in Paris instead!

AVIGNON

587 North Carolina: It is illegal to sell cotton lint or cotton seed at night.

588 Switzerland: It was once against the law to slam your car door.

Gunther loses the very same door his wife slammed in an argument only ten minutes before in the fast lane of the motorway at 120 kph.

589 **A**thens, Greece: A driver's licence can be taken away if the driver is deemed either unbathed or poorly dressed.

590 **H**artford, Connecticut: It is illegal to plant a tree in the street.

Veronica left for work to find the 'Set The Trees Free' organisation had set two trees free illegally in her street.

591 **M**assachusetts: An old ordinance requires a person to have a permit to grow a goatee.

592 **F**lorida: Housewives are not allowed to break more than three dishes a day.

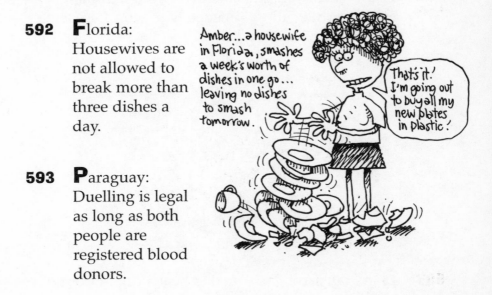

593 **P**araguay: Duelling is legal as long as both people are registered blood donors.

594 Christiansburg, Virginia: It is illegal to spit.

595 Provincetown, Massachusetts: It is illegal to sell suntan oil before noon on a Sunday.

596 Louisiana: Biting someone with your natural teeth is assault, while biting someone with your false teeth is aggravated assault.

597 San Francisco: It is illegal to beat a rug in front of your house.

598 **A**twoodville, Connecticut: People cannot play Scrabble while waiting for a politician to speak.

599 **N**ew York: It is illegal to do anything against the law.

History Never Repeats

600 The carnival made its debut in North America in 1894.

601 The parachute was invented by Leonardo da Vinci in 1515.

602 Cleopatra was Greek, not Egyptian.

603 In 1867, the Russian Czar Alexander II sold Alaska for about $7.2 million to the USA to pay off his gambling debts. At the time, most people thought this was a really bad deal for the USA.

Mamma mia!

If-a I surviva this-a fall I'm-a gonna call-a this a parachute!

Leonardo Da Vinci invents the parachute by accident by taking a fall from his villa roof while hanging out washing.

604 In the Middle Ages, pepper was used for bartering, and it was often more valuable than gold.

605 The oldest restaurant still in business opened in China in 1153.

606 Early bagpipes were made from the livers of sheep.

607 In 1859 in Glamorgan, Wales, a shower of fish fell from the sky.

608 Napoleon constructed his battle plans in a sandbox.

Napoleon plans the Battle of Waterloo in a sandbox.

609 Hawaii officially joined the USA on 14 June 1900.

610 In nineteenth-century Britain, you could be hanged for writing graffiti on Westminster Bridge.

611 Athletes in the ancient Olympics competed in the nude.

612 Money made out of leather was once used in Russia.

613 The Japanese throne has been occupied by a member of the same family since the sixth century. The present emperor is the 125th in succession.

614 The umbrella originated in ancient Egypt, where it was used by the royal family and nobles as a symbol of rank.

615 The first vending machine was invented in 215 BC and was a water dispenser.

616 The Roman Empire existed from about 700 BC, when legend has it that Romulus and Remus founded Rome, to 1453, when the Eastern, or Byzantine, branch of the Empire fell to the Turks.

617 The Vikings reached North America 500 years before the Pilgrims.

618 The Tower of London is currently the home of the British crown jewels. It has been a zoo, an observatory, a mint and a prison.

619 The first product made by Sony was a rice cooker.

620 The dinosaurs were on Earth for almost 150 million years. That is 75 times longer than humans have been on the planet.

621 Napoleon Bonaparte designed the Italian flag.

Napoleon Bonaparte who fancies himself as a flag designer...works on some ideas for the Italian flag.

622 Before 1800, separate shoes for right and left feet were not designed.

Edward tries out the first pair of left and right shoes in 1800.

623 The cigarette lighter was invented before the match.

624 Britain's youngest prime minister was William Pitt in 1783. He was 24 years old.

625 Tea is believed to have been discovered in 2737 BC by a Chinese emperor when some tea leaves accidentally blew into a pot of boiling water.

626 Thomas Sullivan of New York invented the tea bag in 1908.

627 Henry III became king when he was ten months old.

628 Air-filled tyres were used on bicycles before they were used on cars.

629 King George I of England could not speak English.

630 Mexico once had three different presidents in 24 hours.

631 The first email was sent in 1972.

632 A squirrel closed down the New York stock exchange one day in 1987 when it burrowed through a phone line.

633 In ancient Egypt, certain baboons were mummified when they died.

634 The American army tried to train bats to drop bombs during World War II.

635 Sunglasses were invented by the Chinese in the thirteenth century.

636 In 1894, there were only four cars in the USA.

637 **D**enmark has the oldest existing national flag. The flag dates back to the thirteenth century.

The world's oldest existing flag from Denmark is hoisted in a strong breeze for the first time since the thirteenth century.

638 **T**he oldest toy in the world is the doll. It was invented in Greece about 3000 years ago.

639 **I**t was widely believed in the Middle Ages that the heart was the centre of human intelligence.

640 **B**ig Ben, a clock in London, once lost time when a group of birds used the minute hand as a perch.

641 Before 1600, New Year's Day was in March.

642 According to Aristotle, the brain's primary purpose was to cool the blood.

643 In the tenth century, the Grand Vizier of Persia carried his library on 400 trained camels. The camels had to walk in alphabetical order.

644 In ancient Egypt, men and women wore eyeshadow made from crushed beetles.

645 In ancient Japan, public contests were held to see who could fart the loudest and longest.

646 Chrysler built the B-29s that bombed Japan. Mitsubishi built the Zeros that tried to shoot the B-29s down. Both companies now build cars in a joint plant called Diamond Star.

647 The story of Cinderella originated in China.

648 In the nineteenth century, the British navy attempted to disprove the superstition that Friday is an unlucky day to embark on a ship. The keel of a new ship was laid on a Friday, the ship was named HMS *Friday*, she was commanded by a Captain Friday, and she finally went to sea on a Friday. The ship and her crew were never heard of again.

649 In ancient Egypt, monkeys were trained to pick fruit for harvest.

650 The most popular game ever for coin-operated machines is Pac-Man.

651 The formula for cold cream has hardly changed in the 1700 years since it was created by the Roman physician Galen.

652 Queen Elizabeth II of England sent her first email in 1976.

Queen Elizabeth sends her first email... then learns how to surf the internet for great car sites shortly after.

653 Coca-Cola was originally green.

654 Leonardo da Vinci invented scissors.

Leonardo Da Vinci quickly invents the scissors to get him out of one of his other inventions ... ...the parachute.

655 The first television commercial was broadcast in 1941. It cost nine dollars to air.

The first TV commercial cost only $9 to air.

656 The oldest existing governing body, the Althing, operates in Iceland. It was established in AD 930.

657 People started keeping ferrets as pets 500 years before cats were kept as pets.

658 The largest coins were made from copper and were about 1 m (3 ft) long and 60 cm (2 ft) wide. They were used in Alaska in the nineteenth century and were worth $2500.

Wilbur struggles to the store with a huge Alaskan coin.

659 Democracy began 2500 years ago in Athens, Greece.

660 The Sumerians, who lived in the Middle East, invented the wheel in about 3450 BC.

661 Leonardo da Vinci invented an alarm clock that woke you by tickling your feet.

Leonardo Da Vinci is woken by the alarm clock he invented.

662 When tea was first introduced in the American colonies, many people did not know how to drink it. They served the tea leaves with sugar or syrup and threw away the water the leaves had been boiled in.

663 The wheelbarrow was invented in ancient China.

664 Long ago, thermometers were filled with brandy instead of mercury.

665 The first toy balloon, made of vulcanised rubber, was invented in London in 1847.

666 The Olympic torch and flame were invented by Germany for the 1936 Berlin Olympics.

667 Illegal gambling houses in eighteenth-century England employed a person to swallow the dice if there was a police raid.

668 The first message sent over Graham Bell's telephone on 10 March 1876 was 'Mr Watson, come here, I want you'.

669 The Romans were famous for their amazing feasts. They loved to eat exotic foods like snails, swans, crows, horses and peacocks.

670 In the Philippines during the 1500s, the yo-yo was made of stone and used as a weapon.

671 Ancient Egyptians slept on pillows made of stone.

672 Bread was used as an eraser before rubber erasers were invented.

673 In nineteenth-century Britain, you could be hanged for being on a highway with a sooty face.

674 Since its discovery in 1930, Pluto has completed only about 20 per cent of its orbit. The last time Pluto was in its present position was before the American Revolution.

675 Mailing an entire building has been illegal in the USA since 1916 when a man mailed a brick house across Utah to avoid high freight rates.

676 Napoleon Bonaparte was afraid of cats.

The Battle of Waterloo is called off when Napoleon catches sight of a large ginger tom strolling across the battlefield.

677 Tomato sauce was sold in the 1830s as medicine.

678 In *Gulliver's Travels* Jonathan Swift described the two moons of Mars, giving their exact sizes and speeds of rotation. He did this more than 100 years before the moons was discovered.

679 Long ago, clans that wanted to get rid of unpopular people would burn their houses down, hence the expression 'to get fired'.

680 The word 'checkmate' in chess comes from the Persian phrase 'Shah Mat', which means 'the king is dead'.

681   **D**entists in medieval Japan extracted teeth by pulling them out with their fingers.

682   **H**itler was *Time* magazine's Man of the Year in 1938.

683   **C**leopatra sometimes wore a fake beard.

684   **P**rior to World War II, when guards were posted at the fence, anyone could walk up to the front door of the American president's residence, the White House.

685   **E**arly Greeks and Romans used dried watermelons for helmets.

686 The world's first speed limit was introduced in England in 1903. It was 32 km (20 miles) per hour.

687 The first daily television broadcast began in 1936 on the BBC.

688 In nineteenth-century Britain you could be hanged for stealing a spoon.

689 Karate originated in India, but was developed further in China.

Weird

World

Facts

690 The state of Florida is larger than England.

691 The Earth spins
at 1600 km
(1000 miles)
per hour at the
equator.

Hey...
What are you doing?

HANGING ON!
I've just found out
the Earth is
spinning at
1,600 kms
per hour!

692 A lump of pure
gold the size of
a matchbox can
be flattened into
a sheet of gold
the size of a
tennis court.

693 Meteorites slam into the Earth every year.

694 The Earth rotates more slowly on its axis in March than in September.

Meteorites slam into the Earth every year. But where do they hit? Have you ever seen one hit? They always hit somewhere else.

695 Europe is the only continent without a desert.

Believe me! When you've been lost at sea for two weeks...and you try drinking it... Every ocean is just as salty as the next bit.

696 The Pacific Ocean is not as salty as the Atlantic Ocean.

697 Diamonds are flammable.

698 It would take a bullet fired from Earth more than twenty years to reach the sun.

Oh great! Somebody on Earth is doing the test to see how long it takes for a bullet to reach the sun!

699 In Japan, there are vending machines for underwear.

700 In 1980, there was a traffic jam in France that was 176 km (109 miles) long.

701 The Earth flies through space at more than 100 000 km (66 600 miles) per hour.

702 Candles burn better when they are frozen.

703 The largest continent is Asia.

704 Micro-organisms can be found as deep as 3.5 km (2 miles) in the Earth's crust.

705 The South Pole is colder than the North Pole.

706 The USA creates nearly 20 per cent of the world's garbage.

707 The first living creature to orbit the Earth was a dog sent into space by the Russians.

708 All international pilots, no matter where they are from, are required to speak English.

709 In a study by the University of Chicago in 1907, it was found that yellow is the easiest colour to spot.

710 There are more chickens in the world than people.

711 The Greek national anthem has 158 verses.

712 In the Amazon rainforest, 2.5 sq km (1 sq mile) can be home to 3000 species of trees.

713 The moon moves 3.82 cm (1.5 in) away from the Earth every year.

714 Bishop's Rock in the UK is the smallest island in the world.

715 A third of our water gets flushed down the toilet.

716 Damascus in Syria is the oldest inhabited city. It was founded in 753 BC.

717 Australia is the only country that takes up an entire continent.

718 The British flag should only be called the Union Jack when it is on a ship at sea.

719 California, USA, has the fifth largest economy in the world.

720 More than half of the USA coastline is in Alaska.

721 A storm officially becomes a hurricane when it reaches wind speeds of 119 km (74 miles) per hour.

722 In Bangladesh, school children can be jailed for cheating on their exams.

723 Half the world's population is under 25 years old.

724 There are about 1800 thunderstorms occurring on Earth at any given time.

725 The deepest part of the Pacific Ocean is 11 km (6.8 miles).

726 In Australia and the UK, light switches are flicked down for on. In the USA, the switch is flicked up for on.

727 Every year in Sweden a hotel is built out of ice. It melts, then it is rebuilt the next year.

728 **A**lmost half the people on Earth have never made a phone call.

> Mum...Half the people on Earth have never made a phone call.
> And you're one of them!
> So go on!
> Make that call!
> Phone for that PIZZA!
> And make it a large please Mum!

PIZZA MENU

729 **T**here are more than 50 000 earthquakes throughout the world every year.

730 **T**he centre of the Earth is believed to be as hot as the surface of the sun.

731 **T**he most abundant metal in the ground is aluminium.

732 **I**cebergs have been fitted with sailing gear and sailed 3840 km (2400 miles).

> Don't tell me!
> Let me guess!
> I bet you've just sailed in from the Antarctic!

733 **T**he amount of water on Earth is the same now as when the planet formed 4.5 billion years ago.

734 **B**igger raindrops make brighter rainbows.

735 **P**roportionally speaking, the Earth is smoother than a billiard ball.

736 **D**isney World in Florida is twice the size of Manhattan Island.

The Earth was supposed to be as smooth as a billiard ball... But Bob hit a rough patch over North America that sent his 9 ball right off the table.

737 **I**t takes one drop of ocean water more than 1000 years to circulate around the world.

738 **T**he Earth is slightly hotter during a full moon.

Feeling hotter tonight Claude?

No. Why? Am I supposed to? The tin roof's a little warm!

Well the Earth is supposed to be warmer during a full moon so they say!

739 **R**ussia and America are less than 4 km (2.5 miles) apart at their closest point.

740 There are solar-powered pay phones in the Saudi Arabian desert.

741 An estimated 95 per cent of all forms of life that once existed on Earth are now extinct.

742 The international dialling code for Antarctica is 67.

743 Waves in the Pacific Ocean can be up to 34 m (111 ft) high.

744 The Earth is 80 times the size of the moon.

745 It takes eight minutes and 17 seconds for light from the sun to reach Earth.

746 February 1865 is the only month in recorded history that did not have a full moon.

747 The Amazon River pushes lots of water into the Atlantic Ocean. In fact, there is fresh water in the ocean more than 160 km (100 miles) from the mouth of the river.

748 Eighty per cent of people who are hit by lightning are men.

749 The average meteor is no larger than a grain of sand, but it is moving at nearly 48 000 km (30 000 miles) per hour when it enters the atmosphere. This makes it burn so brightly that it is seen as a 'shooting star' from the ground.

750 **A** raindrop falls at about 12 km (7.5 miles) per hour.

751 **D**uring a severe storm the Empire State Building may sway slightly to either side.

Food for Thought

752 Fine-grained volcanic ash is an ingredient in some toothpastes.

753 A person would have to drink more than 12 cups of hot cocoa to consume the amount of caffeine found in one cup of coffee.

754 A favourite dish in old England was lark's tongue.

755 In Vietnam, there is a drink made from lizard blood.

I was about to start cutting these onions... and now I've trod in this awful chewing gum.

Little Rupert couldn't bear to see his Mum cry while cutting onions. So spitting his gum on the floor did the trick. She couldn't cut the onions.

756 Chewing gum can keep a person from crying while cutting onions.

757 Black pepper is the most popular spice in the world.

758 A Tanzanian dish is white ant pie.

759 World eating record #1 is 12 slugs in two minutes.

Tanzanian white ant pie should always be eaten straight away. And never ever left out on a wooden table to cool.

As hard as Walter tried he just couldn't get that 13th slimy slug down to best his previous World Record of 12 slugs in two minutes.

Just one more little slug!

WORLD SLUG EATING CONTEST

760 Eggs are sold on bits of string in Korea.

761 A favourite dish of Indian princes was a sparrow stuffed inside a quail stuffed inside a sand grouse stuffed inside a chicken stuffed inside a peacock stuffed inside a goat stuffed inside a camel and roasted underground until it was tender.

762 **S**ome Amazonian tribes like to barbecue tarantulas and eat them. Apparently they taste like prawns.

How the Jaguar tribe from the Amazon relax around the barbecue.

763 **B**anana plants cannot reproduce themselves. They must be propagated by people.

764 **W**orld eating record #2 is 28 cockroaches in four minutes.

765 **U**nless you have a doctor's note, it is illegal to buy ice cream after 6 p.m. in Newark, New Jersey.

766 **N**achos is the food most often craved by pregnant women.

767 Rat meat sausages were once a delicacy in the Philippines.

768 Canned food was invented in 1813, but a practical can opener was not invented until 1870.

769 Because Hindus do not eat beef, McDonald's in New Delhi makes lamb hamburgers.

770 The blue whale needs to consume 1.5 million calories a day.

771 Genghis Khan killed his brother after an argument over a fish.

772 **W**orld eating record #3 is 60 worms in three minutes.

773 **P**eanuts are one of the ingredients in dynamite.

774 **W**omen swallow and digest most of the lipstick they apply.

775 **R**ubber bands last longer when refrigerated.

Dwayne... keen to impress his friends on their night out to a Japanese Restaurant... ordered large of everything. Including a very large bowl of broiled beetle grubs.

776 **A** Japanese dish is broiled beetle grubs.

777 **W**orld eating record #4 is 13 raw eggs in two seconds.

Walter! 13 RAW EGGS IN TWO SECONDS?

778 The annual harvest of an entire coffee tree makes 450 g (1 lb) of ground coffee.

779 Koalas do not drink water.

780 The first Harley Davidson motorcycle built in 1903 used a tomato can for a carburettor.

781 Bubble gum contains rubber.

782 A cure for whooping cough in old Ireland was sheep's droppings boiled in milk.

783 **A** popular dish in Belize contains mashed and roasted cockroaches.

784 **W**orld eating record #5 is 144 snails in 11 minutes.

785 **A** favourite meal in China is sun-dried maggots.

786 **S**tannous fluoride, which is the cavity fighter found in toothpaste, is made from recycled tin.

787 **M**ost cows give more milk when they listen to music.

788 **M**ore people use blue toothbrushes than red ones.

789 **R**ain contains vitamin B12.

790 **A** Samoan dish is baked bat.

791 **A** favourite dish in Mexico is lamb brain tacos.

792 **W**orld eating record #6 is 12 bananas with skins in four minutes.

793 **I**n Ecuador, people used to eat boiled guinea pig.

794 **T**he microwave was invented in the 1940s after a researcher walked by a radar tube and discovered that a chocolate bar in his pocket had melted.

Hello! Operator? I'd like to find the phone number for a WALTER SMITH please. Do you think I can find his number?? He must have had it disconnected. I'd like to talk to him about a BANANA EATING CONTEST. ...Yes... BANANA. 12 of them in four minutes! With the skins on!

Oh boy! Is it getting warm in here? Or is it just me? My brain is about to explode!

EXPERIMENTAL RADAR

Dr Austin uses the phone in front of the very same radar tube that melted his chocolate bar to tell his fellow researchers of his discovery.

795 **U**ntil the sixteenth century, carrots were black, green, red and purple. Then a Dutch horticulturist discovered some mutant yellow seeds that produced an orange colour.

796 **Y**ou are more likely to be killed by a champagne cork than by a venomous spider.

Despite a venomous spider being on the loose at the wedding ...
It was the bride's father with a champagne bottle they really had to fear.

797 **E**ating an apple will make you feel more awake in the morning than drinking a cup of coffee will.

798 **A**stronauts are not allowed to eat beans before they go into space because passing wind in a spacesuit damages it.

799 Most lipsticks contain fish scales.

800 A favourite dish in Norway is beef blood pudding.

Erik from Norway tries out his
first beef blood pudding.

801 World eating record #7 is 100 maggots in five minutes.

Wacky Word Facts

802 No words in the English language rhyme with month, orange, silver or purple.

803 'Go' is the shortest sentence in the English language.

804 The word 'paradise' was once the Persian word for a royal amusement park.

805 The Cambodian alphabet is the largest. It has 74 letters.

806 The Hawaiian alphabet consists of only 12 letters.

807 The longest word in English is 'pneumonoultramicroscopicsilicovolcanoconiosis'.

808 Aardvark means 'earth pig'.

809 The only 15-letter word that can be spelled without repeating a letter is 'uncopyrightable'.

810 The name 'jeep' comes from the abbreviation used in the army for the general purpose vehicle, GP.

811 The Inuit (Eskimos) have 20 different words for snow.

812 **D**r Seuss invented the word 'nerd'.

813 **T**he computer term 'bug' originated in the days when computers were made from vacuum tubes. Bugs liked to live in the warm tubes and this sometimes caused short circuits.

814 **'Z**orro' is Spanish for 'fox'.

The great Mexican super hero...Zorro (the fox)

815 **T**he word 'news' is actually an acronym for the four compass points (<u>n</u>orth, <u>e</u>ast, <u>w</u>est and <u>s</u>outh).

816 **A**ttics were invented in Attica.

817 **T**he first word spoken on the moon was 'Okay'.

When I told him the Lunar Module was out of fuel and we couldn't bring him back to Earth...You know what he said? ...OKAY!

He said OKAY?

He must have left his hearing aid batteries at home on his dressing table!

818 The oldest word in the English language is 'town'.

819 The word 'diastima' means having a gap between your teeth.

820 The gorilla's scientific name is *Gorilla gorilla*.

821 The longest one-syllable word in the English language is 'screeched'.

822 More people in China speak English than in the USA.

823 The word 'Mrs' cannot be written in full.

824 The dot over the letter 'i' is called the tittle.

825 Butterflies used to be called 'flutterbys'.

826 'Aloha' means both 'goodbye' and 'hello' in Hawaiian.

827 The 'sixth sick sheik's sixth sheep's sick' is the toughest tongue-twister in the English language.

828 **A** 'spat' is a baby oyster.

829 **T**he word 'queueing' is the only English word with five consecutive vowels.

830 **N**ewton is the most common place name in Britain. There are 150 places with that name.

831 **I**n England in the 1880s, 'pants' was considered a dirty word.

832 **'D**reamt' is the only English word that ends in the letters 'mt'.

833 **'O**f' is the only word in which an 'f' is pronounced like a 'v'.

834 **A** pregnant goldfish is called a twit.

835 'Bookkeeper' and 'bookkeeping' are the only words in the English language with three consecutive sets of double letters.

836 The word 'taxi' is spelled the same in English, German, French, Swedish and Portuguese.

837 The most used letter in the English alphabet is 'e', and 'q' is the least used.

838 The word 'karaoke' means 'empty orchestra'.

839 The sentence 'the quick brown fox jumps over the lazy dog' uses every letter in the alphabet.

Strange Science

840 **G**lass is made from sand.

Come and make sandcastles Edward!

Come in for a swim Eddie!

Now... I'll just calculate how many glass bottles could be made out of all of the sand on every beach in the world!

841 **G**lass, which looks like a solid, is actually a very slow moving liquid.

While the other kids took their buckets and spades to the beach... Edward the nerd took his calculator.

842 **A**n iceberg contains more heat than a lighted match.

Well... If an iceberg contains more heat than a lighted match... I guess that eventually that heat is going to melt that iceberg!

843 **V**elcro was invented by a person who studied the burrs that clung to his dog's coat after a walk.

844 White light is a mixture of all the colours in the spectrum.

845 Eleanor Roosevelt received a telegram from the 1939 World's Fair in New York that used only the power from electric eels.

846 Scientists are genetically engineering a breed of goat that will produce milk that can be turned into spider silk, then spun into ultra-strong ropes.

847 Some forms of primitive life can survive anywhere that water is found, even in boiling water or ice.

848 The sound of a whip cracking is actually a mini sonic boom that occurs when the tip of the whip breaks the sound barrier.

849 Using nanotechnology, a microscopic guitar with strings has been made. It is no larger than a blood cell.

850 The temperature on the moon can drop by up to 260°C (500°F) at night.

I've heard the temperature on the moon can drop by up to 260°c at night. So I'm packing a spare jumper to take with me!

851 During one four-year period, inventor Thomas Edison registered almost 300 patents.

852 John Logie Baird made the first television in 1924 using cardboard, scrap wood, needles, string and other materials.

853 More than a thousand new insects are discovered every year.

Geoffrey discovers some of the one thousand or so new insects found every year on the windshield of his car at 100 kph on the motorway.

854 In 1889, the commissioner of the United States Patent Office announced that 'Everything that can be invented, has been invented'.

855 Toilet paper was invented in New York in 1857.

856 The first video-cassette recorder was built in 1956. It was the size of an upright piano.

857 A cross between a goat and a sheep is called a 'geep'.

858 Thomas Edison was afraid of the dark.

Maybe Thomas Edison invented the light bulb because he was afraid of the dark.

859 The computer term 'byte' is short for 'by eight'.

860 Arecibo observatory in Puerto Rico has one of the largest radio telescopes in the world. It is over 300 m (1000 ft) across and could pick up the signal from a mobile phone on Jupiter.

Let's see just how well that Arecibo radio telescope works down there on Earth. I'm going to order a pizza to be delivered on this mobile phone from a store in Puerto Rico.

861 English chemist John Walker never patented his invention of matches because he felt such an important tool should be public property.

862 Florence Nightingale did not believe in bacteria.

863 Sir Isaac Newton invented the cat flap.

Oh Kitty! My poor little Kitty! Just like why an apple falls from a tree ...I have a theory for why you hit that door and bounced off. You need a catflap in the door that opens my friend!

864 The world's smallest motor has recently been built at the Berkeley campus of the University of California. Three hundred of the motors could line up on the stump left when you cut a hair.

865 Honey is sometimes used in antifreeze mixtures and in the centre of golf balls.

866 The Eiffel Tower always leans away from the sun because heat makes the metal expand.

867 You can start a fire by using a lens-shaped piece of ice and concentrating a beam of sunlight onto flammable material.

868 The electric chair was invented by a dentist.

I thought to myself... there's something about this dentist that gives me the creeps. Perhaps it was the look on his face. ...The hard uncomfortable wooden seat... the belts that tightened around me ... or the talk of exceptionally large power bills.. or was it unusual that a dentist should talk about inventing ... THE ELECTRIC CHAIR?

869 The first stethoscope was made in 1816 with a roll of paper.

I can't hear a heartbeat my good fellow! All I can hear is a sound like a paper tube crumbling!

CRUNCH

I think you're in trouble

Me too!

870 Cat urine glows under a black light.

871 Hot water freezes more quickly than cold water.

Patent Mania

872 Patent no. GB2272154 is for a ladder to enable spiders to climb out of a bath. The ladder comprises a thin, flexible strip of latex rubber that follows the inner contours of the bath. A suction pad on the ladder is attached to the top of the bath.

873 Patent no. GB2060081 is for a horse-powered minibus. The horse walks along a conveyor belt in the middle of the bus. This drives the wheels via a gearbox. A thermometer under the horse's collar is connected to the vehicle instrument panel. The driver can signal to the horse using a handle, which brings a mop into contact with the horse.

874 Patent no. GB2172200 is for an umbrella for wearing on the head. The support frame is designed not to mess up the wearer's hair.

Well...The best features of this new umbrella are that it doesn't mess up my hair... and it leaves me two hands to shop!

RAIN? Oh no...you can't use it in the rain! You'll get wet!

875 Patent no. GB2289222 is for a fart-collecting device. It comprises a gas-tight collecting tube for insertion into the rectum of the subject. The tube is connected to a gas-tight collecting bag. The end of the tube inserted into the subject is covered with a gauze filter and a gas permeable bladder.

876 Patent no. US6325727 is for an underwater golf swing training device. The device has a hydrodynamically adjustable paddle that can be altered manually. This provides variable resistance to the user as he swings the device through the water.

Bob, trying out his new underwater golf swing training device, tries for the bunker but only manages the side of the smimming pool.

877 Patent no. GB2267208 is for a portable seat that is worn on a waist-belt. The seat cushion can pivot from a stowed position to a seating position.

878 Patent no. US4233942 is for a device for protecting the ears of a long-haired dog from becoming soiled by food while it is eating. A tube contains each of the dog's ears. The tubes are held away from the dog's mouth and food while it eats.

879 Patent no. WO9701384 is for a leash for walking an imaginary pet. It has a preformed shape and supports a simulated pet harness and collar. A micro loudspeaker in the collar is connected to an integrated circuit in the handle, to produce a variety of barks and growls.

880 Patent no. GB1453920 is for rolled-up fire curtains at roof level on a skyscraper. When a fire starts, the curtains are released to cover the building and suffocate the fire.

881 Patent no. US5971829 is for a motorised ice-cream cone. The cone spins while you lick the ice cream.

882 Patent no. US2760763 is for an egg beater that beats the egg within its shell.

883 Patent no. US6637447 is for the 'Beerbrella'. This is a tiny umbrella that clips onto a beer bottle, keeping the sun off the beverage.

884 Patent no. WO98/21939 is for deer ears. To use, simply place the deer ears on your head and swivel your new ears in the direction you would like to hear.

885 Patent no. US3150831 is for a birthday cake candle extinguisher.

886 Patent no. US5713081 is for three-legged pantihose. When there is a run in the stocking, you simply rotate your leg into the spare

hose. The damaged hose is then tucked into a pocket in the crotch of the pantihose.

887 Patent no. US5719656 is for earless eyewear. Stick the self-adhesive magnets on to each side of your head. The eyewear frames contain internal magnets that hold on to the magnets on your temples.

888 Patent no. US4022227 is for a three way comb-over to cover a bald head. Just let your hair grow long at the sides, then divide it into three sections and comb it over your bald head one section at a time.

889 Patent no. US4344424 is for a mouth cage that is designed to allow you to breathe and speak but not eat.

890 Patent no. US4872422 is for a pet petter. This is an electronic device consisting of an eye that spots your pet and signals the electronic motors to activate the petting arm. The arm is tipped with a human-like hand for added realism.

891 Patent no. USD342712 is for a frame that clamps around your pet's waist and supports a clear plastic tent-like structure that keeps your pet dry in the rain. There are air holes in the tent.

892 Patent no. US6557994 is for a way to hang eyeglasses on your face. You use body piercing studs. Pierce your eyebrows and hang your glasses from the studs. There is also a design that works with a nose bridge stud.

893 Patent no. US6266930 is for a 'Squabble Shield'. The shield is a shatterproof, clear plexiglass wall that fits in the middle of the back seat of a family car. It keeps children apart, and from squabbling, while the parent is driving.

894   Patent no. US4825469 is for a fully inflatable motorcycle suit. When the rider falls off the bike, the suit swells with compressed gas until it covers the head, arms, torso and legs, protecting the rider from damage.

895   Patent no. US4365889 is for a wristband with an absorbent pad. People with colds can wipe their noses on it. It also has a cover that flips down, keeping all the nasties inside.

896   Patent no. US4299921 is for the 'Smell This' breath mask. You check if your breath is smelly by placing the mask on your face, then breathing out through your mouth and breathing in through your nose.

897 Patent no. US3842343 is for mud flaps to keep mud from flying up the back of your shoes.

898 Patent no. US6704666 is for the 'Speak & Swing', which is a motorised golf club selection system. You simply speak to your golf bag, telling it which club you want, and the club automatically pops up.

899 Patent no. US5372954 is for the 'Wig Flipper'. A wig is placed on a large spring and attached to a small cap. The wig and spring are then compressed, locked onto the cap and placed on your head. When you push the spring release button the hairpiece will jump into the air.

900 Patent no. US6600372 is for the 'Spitting Duck'. This device fits most toilets and, instead of using toilet paper, you lift the duck's bill and a strategically placed nozzle will spray your bottom with the cleaning formula.

901 Patent US5352633 is for the 'Arm Mitten', which the driver of a car wears on one arm. This protects the arm from sunburn when the elbow rests on the window ledge.

902 Patent no. US6630345 is for the 'Wonder Butt Bra', which lifts, supports and shapes a person's butt, giving it a desirable shape. It is fully adjustable to fit all sizes of butts.

903 Patent no. US5848443 is for the 'Travel Relief'. This is a padded toilet for use while driving. It even flushes.

904 Patent US5375340 is for 'Cool Shoes', which are air-conditioned shoes that have a mini-network of heat exchange coils built into the heels. With each step, the wearer activates the compressor chamber, which forces cool air up into the shoe via a rubber bladder in the sole.

905 Patent US5130161 is for the 'Life Expectancy Watch'. You program the watch by answering questions about your lifestyle. Your estimated remaining time on Earth is displayed in years, months, days and hours.

Hilarious Humans

906 Every person has a unique tongue print.

907 Your right lung takes in more air than your left lung does.

908 A woman's heart beats faster than a man's.

909 The inventor of Vaseline ate a spoonful of the stuff every morning.

910 Albert Einstein never wore socks.

911 **A**stronauts get taller when they are in space.

912 **P**eople photo-copying their butts is the cause of 23 per cent of all photocopier malfunctions.

913 **I**t is impossible to cry in space because of the lack of gravity.

914 **B**ill Gates' house was designed using a Macintosh computer.

915 **O**nly one per cent of bacteria are harmful to humans.

916 **Y**our eyes use 25 per cent of your brain power.

917 In Brazil in 1946, a woman gave birth to decaplets (ten children). She had eight girls and two boys.

918 To be a NASA astronaut your height cannot exceed 182 cm (6 ft).

919 There are four basic tastes the human tongue can detect. Salty and sweet are tasted on the tip of the tongue, bitter is tasted at the base of the tongue, and sour is tasted along the sides of the tongue.

920 The average person blinks about 24 times per minute or about 12.5 million times per year.

921 Wedding rings are worn on the fourth finger of the left hand because people used to believe that the vein in this finger goes directly to the heart.

922 The average human dream lasts two to three seconds.

923 Twenty-five per cent of your bones are located in your feet.

924 Albert Einstein's eyes were auctioned in 1994 after being stored in a safety deposit box since his death in 1955.

925 The numbers of births in India each year exceeds the entire population of Australia (20 million).

926 The world's human population was only five million in 5000 BC.

927 If the population of China lined up and you had to walk the length of the line, you would be walking forever because of all the new births.

928 Every year 4000 people injure themselves with teapots.

929 The measurement from your wrist to your elbow is the same measurement as your foot.

930 Nearly ten per cent of American households dress their pets in Halloween costumes.

931   **A**rteries carry blood away from the heart. Veins carry blood towards the heart.

932   **A**ccording to a study by the Economic Research Service, 27 per cent of all food produced in Western nations ends up in garbage bins. Yet 1.2 billion people in the world are underfed.

933   **G**irls have more taste buds than boys do.

934   **T**here are only 200 family names in China for a population of well over a billion.

935   **Y**ou breathe in and out about 23 000 times a day.

936 The average height of people in Western nations has increased by 10 cm (4 in) in the last 150 years.

937 Roy Sullivan of Virginia, USA, has been hit by lightning seven times.

938 One out of twenty people has an extra rib.

939 Douglas Bader was born in London in 1910. He flew for the Royal Air Force in World War II but both his legs were amputated after his aeroplane crashed. He became a flight leader and was instrumental in the Battle of Britain. He attained 23 combat victories by the summer of 1941, making him the fifth highest scoring ace in the RAF.

940 New Zealand was the first country to give women the vote.

941 The average person has at least seven dreams a night.

942 A corpse left out in warm weather will be reduced to a skeleton in about nine days.

943 The most common name in the world is Mohammed.

944 In 1973, a confectionery salesman was buried in a coffin made of chocolate in accordance with his dying wishes.

945 Taste buds last about ten days. Of course, your body is making new ones all the time.

946 In India, people wear masks on the back of their heads when they go outside. This confuses tigers because they like to attack from the rear.

947 The Beijing Duck Restaurant in China can seat 9000 people.

948 Colour blindness is ten times more common in men than in women.

949 Humans spend a third of their lives sleeping.

950 **R**obots in Japan pay union dues.

951 **T**he Mbuti Pygmies are among the shortest people in the world. The average height for a man is 137 cm (4 ft 6 in) tall.

952 **L**ack of sleep will kill a person faster than starvation will.

953 **B**oanthropy is a disease that makes a person believe he is an ox.

954 **A** person cannot taste food unless it is mixed with saliva. For example, if salt is placed on a dry tongue, the taste buds will not be able to taste it. As soon as a drop of saliva is added and the salt is dissolved, the person tastes the salt.

955 Tibetans and Mongolians put salt in their tea instead of sugar.

956 Your tongue is the strongest muscle in your body.

957 Mosquitoes are more attracted to people who have recently eaten bananas.

958 Masai tribesman leave their dead out for wild animals to eat.

959 There are villages in Papua New Guinea that are only a twenty-minute walk apart, but the villagers speak different languages.

960 The Neanderthal's brain was bigger than your brain is.

961 **A** pair of leather shoes can supply enough nourishment for a person for about a week.

962 **N**apoleon Bonaparte's penis was put up for auction in 1972. It did not sell. It was later purchased for $3800.

963 **T**he average person is 6.2 mm (0.25 in) taller at night.

964 **T**he Inuit (Eskimos) use fridges to stop their food from freezing.

965 **T**he only part of the human body that has no blood supply is the cornea of the eye. It takes in oxygen directly from the air.

966 Fingernails live for three to six months. They grow nearly 4 cm (1.5 in) a year.

967 A 10 cm (4 in) lock of Beethoven's hair sold at Sotheby's for £4000 in 1994.

968 Midgets and dwarfs usually have normal-size children.

969 In the USA, deaf people have safer driving records than people who can hear.

970 Forty per cent of dog and cat owners carry pictures of their pets in their wallets.

971 Only 55 per cent of Americans know that the sun is a star.

972 Human skin sheds continually. The outer layer of skin is entirely replaced every 28 days.

973 In 1980, a Las Vegas hospital suspended workers for betting on when patients would die.

974 In Los Angeles, there are more cars than people.

975 When D. H. Lawrence died, his ashes were mixed with cement, then used to make his girlfriend's mantelpiece.

976 The body of Charlie Chaplin was stolen in 1978 from a Swiss graveyard and held for ransom. The sum demanded was 600 000 francs.

977 Even if up to 80 per cent of it is removed, the human liver can continue to function and it will grow back to its original size.

978 Manhole covers are always round because they rest on a lip that is smaller than the cover. This means the cover cannot fit through the opening on any angle. A square or rectangular cover could fall through.

Gavin's head was square. So he found it difficult to fit through round manholes.

BONK

BUMP

CLUNK

979 Your sense of smell is about five per cent as strong as a dog's.

What's wrong? These sneakers smell perfectly fine to me.

Oh please! You're going to make me sick!

980 The pupil of a human eye will expand as much as 45 per cent when it sees something pleasing.

981 Tibetans drink tea made with salt and rancid yak butter.

982 Even the cleverest person only uses one per cent of the English language.

983 Men sweat 40 per cent more than women do.

984 The greatest number of descendants belonged to Samuel Mast. When he died in 1992, at the age of 96, he had 824 living descendants.

985 The creator of the waffle iron did not like waffles.

986 Forty-two per cent of people urinate in the shower.

987 The object that is most often choked on by Americans is the toothpick.

988 The average person laughs 15 times a day.

989 Chinese people make up more than 20 per cent of the world's population.

990 The largest cell in the human body is the ovum, the female reproductive cell.

991 During your life, you will eat an average of 70 insects and ten spiders while sleeping.

Cecil leaves the bedroom window open and swallows most of his expected life's quota of 70 insects and ten spiders while he sleeps

992 The longest beard on a woman was 27.9 cm (11 in).

993 Japanese speakers learn Spanish faster than they learn English. English speakers learn Spanish faster than they learn Japanese.

994 The most productive mother gave birth to 69 children.

995 In Albania, nodding your head means no and shaking it means yes.

Hello! I appear to be lost! Can you tell me please.. Is this the way to the AIRPORT?

OK! I realise you don't speak much English But you're nodding your head.. So you must mean.. YES.

While asking an Albanian lady for directions Austin is unaware that in Albania people shake their heads for yes.. and nod for no. Austin ends up in neighbouring Serbia instead of the Airport.

996 While you are reading this sentence, 50 000 cells in your body will have been replaced by new cells.

997 A baby excretes its own weight in faeces every 60 hours.

While sneezing can be known to break a rib... Sneezing while walking down stairs can be much more dangerous.

998 Although an extremely rare occurrence, sneezing too hard can fracture a rib.

999 The average human body contains enough fat to make seven bars of soap.

Hey Barb! You're looking great! You've lost so much weight.

I know Cheryl. And I'd like you to have some of it.

Cheryl finds out that there's enough fat in the human body to make seven bars of soap.

1000 Babies are born without kneecaps. Kneecaps do not appear until a child is two years old.

1001 The oldest known person lived to 122 years of age.

Bob...known to his friends at the nursing home as 'Methusela' tries to blow and make a wish...But can't get close enough to the cake for the raging inferno created by the 120 birthday candles.